LIFE CYCLE OF A...

Turtle

Revised and Updated

Ron Fridell
and
Patricia Walsh

Heinemann Library
Chicago, IL

www.heinemannraintree.com

Visit our website to find out more information about Heinemann-Raintree books.

To order:

☎ Phone 888-454-2279

🖥 Visit www.heinemannraintree.com to browse our catalog and order online.

Edited by Adrian Vigliano, Harriet Milles, and Diyan Leake
Designed by Kimberly R. Miracle and Tony Miracle
Original illustrations ©Capstone Global Library Limited 1998, 2009
Illustrated by David Westerfield
Picture research by Tracy Cummins and Heather Mauldin
Originated by Chroma Graphics (Overseas) Pte. Ltd.
Printed in China by South China Printing Company Ltd.

13 12 11 10 09
10 9 8 7 6 5 4 3 2 1

New edition ISBNs: 978 1 4329 2532 1 (hardcover)
                   978 1 4329 2549 9 (paperback)

The Library of Congress has cataloged the first edition as follows:
Fridell, Ron.
  Life cycle of a - turtle / by Ron Fridell, Patricia Walsh.
    p. cm.
    Includes bibliographical references (p.) and index.
    ISBN 1-58810-096-0   ISBN 978-1-58810-096-2
  1. Turtles—Life cycles—Juvenile literature. [1. Turtles.]
  I. Walsh, Patricia, 1951- II. Title.
  QL666.C5 F68 2001
  597.92—dc21

Acknowledgments

The author and publisher are grateful to the following for permission to reproduce copyright material: ©Pat & Chuck Blackley p. 19; Corbis p. 18 (©Corbis/Gary W. Carter); Getty Images pp. 4 (©Jeff Hunter), 6 (©George Grall), 7 (©Medford Taylor), 22 (©Joel Sartore), 23 (©Rich Addicks); Jupiter Images p. 16 (©Royalty free); ©Dwight Kuhn p. 25; Nature Picture Library pp. 12, 17, **28 top right** (©Lynn M. Stone); Photo Researchers, Inc. pp. **13**, **28 bottom** (©Paul J. Fusco); Photoshot pp. **8**, **14**, **15**, **20**, **21**, **29 top left**, **29 top right**, **29 bottom** (©Bruce Coleman/Joe McDonald), **9**, **10** (©Bruce Coleman/Edward R. Degginger), **11**, **28 top left** (©Bruce Coleman/Robert L. Dunne), **26** (©Bruce Coleman); Visuals Unlimited Inc. pp. **5** (©Rob & Ann Simpson), **24** (©Jim Merli), **27** (©Jack Dermid).

Cover photograph of a box turtle reproduced with permission of age fotostock (©Arco Images/Richard H).

We would like to thank Michael Bright for his invaluable help in the preparation of this book.

Every effort has been made to contact copyright holders of any material reproduced in this book. Any omissions will be rectified in subsequent printings if notice is given to the publisher.

Contents

Some words are shown in bold, **like this**. You can find out what they mean by looking in the glossary.

Meet the Turtles

This is a photo of a sea turtle.

Turtles are **reptiles**. There are many different kinds of turtles. They live in water or on land. Turtles walk slowly on land, but they swim fast in water.

Eggs

3 months

1 year

The turtle's tough shell protects its soft body.

Every turtle has a shell. The top of the shell is called a **carapace**. The bottom of the shell is called a **plastron**.

Life on Land

Box turtles always live near streams or ponds

The turtle in this book is a box turtle. Box turtles live in woodlands, pastures, or meadows.

Eggs

3 months

1 year

The carapace is the top part of the turtle's shell.

The box turtle's **carapace** is brown or black. This turtle's shell and scaly skin have orange and red spots.

1-5 years

5-7 years

30 years

Nesting and Laying Eggs

The female turtle needs soft, sandy soil to make a nest for her eggs.

The female box turtle digs a nest with her back feet. It takes her many hours to dig a smooth, shallow hole for her eggs.

Eggs

3 months

1 year

She lays a **clutch** of four to six eggs in the nest. She might lay another clutch three or four weeks later.

The box turtle's eggs are white.

1-5 years

5-7 years

30 years

The turtle uses her back legs to cover up her eggs with soil.

The mother turtle carefully covers her eggs with soil. The soil keeps the eggs warm and wet until they are ready to hatch.

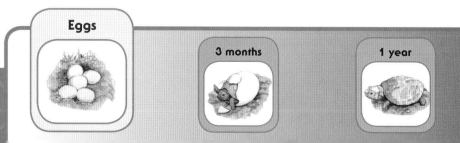

Eggs

3 months

1 year

A turtle egg is about as long as your thumb.

The eggs in the nest are oval shaped.
Inside each egg, a tiny turtle is growing.

1-5 years

5-7 years

30 years

Hatching

The baby box turtle has to chip its way out of the egg.

After two or three months, the tiny turtle is ready to **hatch**. It uses the **eggtooth** on the tip of its **beak** to chip away bits of shell.

Eggs

3 months

1 year

A baby turtle that has just hatched from an egg is called a hatchling.

It takes many days for the turtle to break out of its shell. The tiny turtle **hatchling** is about the size of a nickel.

1-5 years

5-7 years

30 years

Young Turtle

The hungry young turtle eats during the day.

The young box turtle grows about half the length of your thumb each year. As its body grows, its shell gets bigger, too.

Eggs

3 months

1 year

The young turtle likes to eat worms and **slugs**.

The turtle crunches snails and **insects**. It nibbles berries and roots. It has no teeth, but it can bite with its jaws.

1-5 years   5-7 years   30 years

Turtles like to bathe their bodies in water.

The turtle is most active in the early morning and late afternoon. It hunts for food and soaks in shallow water.

Eggs

3 months

1 year

This turtle is keeping cool in the wet leaves.

In hot weather, the turtle sits under logs or leaves to stay cool. In cool weather, it sits in the Sun to get warm.

1-5 years

5-7 years

30 years

Hibernating

The turtle cannot find food when the weather turns cold.

In the winter months, the turtle **hibernates**. It buries itself in leaves and soft dirt, or crawls into a hole. Its heart slows down, and it stops eating.

Eggs

3 months

1 year

The turtle comes out of hibernation in spring.

The turtle hibernates all through winter. When the weather turns warm again, it digs its way out. It starts to look for food.

1-5 years

5-7 years

30 years

Adult Turtle

When it is fully grown, the turtle will be four to six inches long.

The turtle is an adult when it is about 7 years old. It will slowly grow for about 20 years.

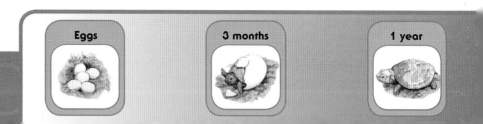

Eggs

3 months

1 year

Some turtles have lived
as long as 100 years.

If the turtle escapes **predators** and stays
healthy, it will live for many years. The
average turtle lives 30 to 40 years.

1-5 years

5-7 years

30 years

Turtles in Danger

Skunks, opossums, foxes, and snakes all like to eat turtles.

When the turtle is threatened by a **predator**, it pulls in its head, legs, and tail. Then it closes up its shell as tight as it can.

Eggs

3 months

1 year

Many turtles get crushed by cars and trucks.

Roads and fields can be dangerous places for the turtle. Its shell is no match for car wheels or a farmer's sharp plow.

1-5 years

5-7 years

30 years

Homes in Danger

Turtles need a safe place to live, with grass and trees.

The turtle might lose its home if people build houses and roads in its **habitat**. When there is no **open land**, the turtle cannot find food or a place to lay its eggs.

Eggs

3 months

1 year

Some people take turtles to keep or sell as pets.

The turtle might also be taken from its home. If the turtle is left alone, it will live a long time in the wild.

1-5 years

5-7 years

30 years

Mating

Box turtles need to be around 13 years old before they can mate.

Adult turtles do not pay much attention to each other until it is time to **mate**. The male turtle **fertilizes** the female turtle's eggs.

Eggs

3 months

1 year

Now the female turtle is ready to lay her eggs.

A month or two later, she looks for a safe place to dig her nest and lay her eggs.

1-5 years

5-7 years

30 years

Life Cycle

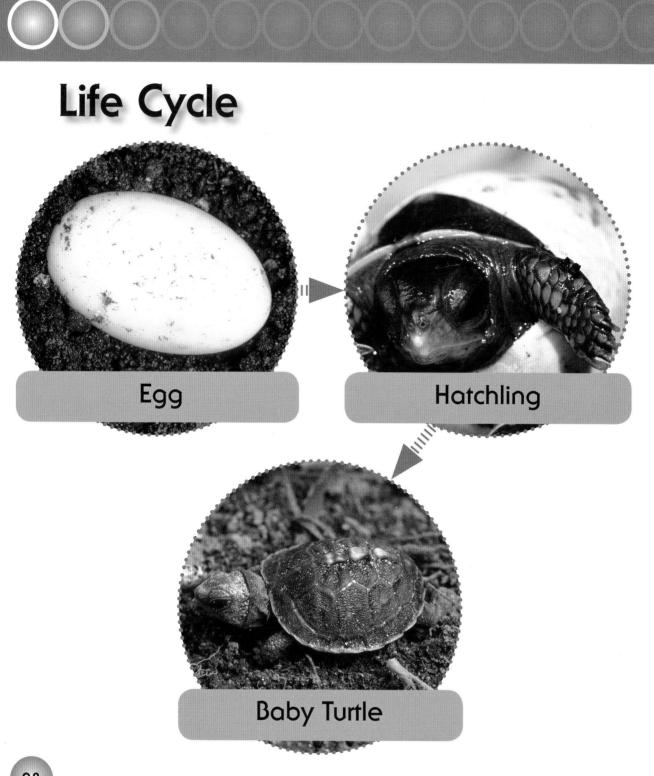

Egg

Hatchling

Baby Turtle

Young Turtle

7 Years Old

30 Years Old

Fact File

- A turtle cannot walk out of its shell. Its backbone and ribs are part of its **carapace**.

- Turtles are the oldest living group of **reptiles**. They have been on Earth since the time of the dinosaurs.

- Few **hatchlings** grow to be adult turtles. Many are eaten by birds, **rodents**, or skunks.

- In many states, it is against the law to take a wild turtle home as a pet.

- There are 250 kinds of turtles on Earth today.

Glossary

beak part of a turtle's mouth that is used to cut food

carapace top part of a turtle's shell

clutch nest of eggs

eggtooth small, sharp bump on the beak of a baby turtle, used to break the eggshell when hatching

fertilize when cells from a male turtle join with eggs from a female to make baby turtles

habitat place where an animal lives

hatch to break out of an egg

hatchling baby turtle

hibernate to spend the winter as if in a deep sleep

insect small animal that has six legs, a body with three main parts, and wings

mate when a male and female come together to produce babies

open land clear space; countryside

plastron bottom part of a turtle shell

predator animal that eats other animals

reptile cold-blooded animal that creeps or crawls and has scaly skin, such as a snake, lizard, turtle, or alligator

rodent gnawing animal, such as a rat, mouse, or squirrel

slug animal like a snail, that has no shell

More Books to Read

Blomquist, Christopher. *Box Turtles (Library of Turtles and Tortoises)*. New York: PowerKids Press, 2004.

Stille, Darlene, Elizabeth Laskey, and Carol Baldwin. *Sea Turtles (Sea Creatures)* Chicago: Heinemann Library, 2003.

Stone, Lynn M. *Box Turtles (Nature Watch Series)*. Minneapolis: Lerner Publishing Group, 2007.

Index